Profiles of the Presidents

MARTIN VAN BUREN

★ ★ ★

Profiles of the Presidents

MARTIN VAN BUREN

by Robin S. Doak

Content Adviser: Patricia West, Ph.D., Martin Van Buren National Historic Site, Kinderhook, New York

Reading Adviser: Dr. Linda D. Labbo, Department of Reading Education, College of Education, The University of Georgia

COMPASS POINT BOOKS ✶ MINNEAPOLIS, MINNESOTA

Compass Point Books
151 Good Counsel Drive
P.O. Box 669
Mankato, MN 56002-0669

Visit Compass Point Books on the Internet at *www.compasspointbooks.com*
or e-mail your request to *custserv@compasspointbooks.com*

Photographs ©: White House Collection, Courtesy White House Historical Association, cover, 1, 37 (bottom); Stock Montage, 7, 9, 12, 17, 36, 42, 54 (left); Francis G. Mayer/Corbis, 8; Lombard Antiquarian Maps & Prints, 10, 13, 27, 29, 31, 48 (top), 55 (bottom left), 57 (left); Hulton/Archive by Getty Images, 11, 20, 21, 22, 24, 25, 30, 33, 37 (top), 45, 47, 48 (bottom), 54 (right), 55 (right, all), 56 (top right), 57 (right), 59 (left and bottom right); Library of Congress, 14, 18, 32, 43, 55 (top left); N. Carter/North Wind Picture Archives, 15; North Wind Picture Archives, 23; Bettmann/Corbis, 26, 35, 38; Courtesy Martin Van Buren National Historic Park, Kinderhook, New York, 40, 56 (left); Woolaroc Museum, Bartlesville, Oklahoma, 41; Lee Snider/Corbis, 49, 50; Department of Rare Books and Special Collections, University of Rochester Library, 56 (bottom right); Texas Library & Archives Commission, 58; Bruce Burkhardt/Corbis, 59 (top right).

Editors: E. Russell Primm, Emily J. Dolbear, Melissa McDaniel, and Catherine Neitge
Photo Researcher: Svetlana Zhurkina
Photo Selector: Heidi Schoof
Designer/Page Production: The Design Lab/Les Tranby
Cartographer: XNR Productions, Inc.

Library of Congress Cataloging-in-Publication Data
Doak, Robin S. (Robin Santos), 1963–
   Martin Van Buren / by Robin S. Doak.
      p. cm.— (Profiles of the presidents)
Summary: A passion for politics—Early years—The young politician—Onto the national scene—
The President's right-hand man—A difficult presidency—Defeat and retirement.
Includes bibliographical references and index.
   ISBN-13: 978-0-7565-0256-0
   ISBN-10: 0-7565-0256-X
   1. Van Buren, Martin, 1782–1862—Juvenile literature. 2. Presidents—United States—Biography—
Juvenile literature. [1. Van Buren, Martin, 1782–1862. 2. Presidents.] I. Title. II. Series.
   E387 .D63 2003
   973.5'7'092—dc21   2002010002

Table of Contents

★   ★   ★

*NOTE: In this book, words that are defined in the glossary are in **bold** the first time they appear in the text.*

A Passion for Politics

★   ★   ★

Martin Van Buren loved politics. For nearly sixty years, he devoted himself to serving his state and his nation. During his long career, Van Buren reshaped the U.S. government. He and others of his time believed that all people should have their voices heard. Van Buren helped found the Democratic Party. He also became the most powerful person in New York politics.

In 1836, Van Buren was elected the nation's eighth president. He was the first U.S. president who was born an American citizen. Previous presidents had been born before the United States had gained independence from Great Britain. Also, unlike some earlier presidents, he was not from a rich family.

Van Buren faced great challenges as president. His term was marred by one problem after another. Yet Van Buren served his nation well.

◄ *President Martin Van Buren*

Early Years

★ ★ ★

Martin Van Buren was born on December 5, 1782, in the small town of Kinderhook, New York. The town, located in the Hudson River valley, was home to many people of **Dutch** descent. Both Van Buren's mother and father, Maria and Abraham, traced their roots back to the Netherlands. As children, Martin and his brothers and sisters spoke Dutch at home.

Van Buren grew ▶ up in the Hudson River valley.

The Van Buren family farmhouse in Kinderhook, New York

Abraham Van Buren owned a farm and a small tavern in Kinderhook. Despite Abraham's two jobs, the Van Burens often had a tough time making ends meet. Martin and his brothers and sisters pitched in to help. Sometimes they worked on the farm, planting, weeding, or picking vegetables. At other times, they helped out in the family's busy little tavern.

The Van Burens ▲
owned a tavern in
Albany like the one
pictured here.

The tavern was located near a main road between New York City and Albany, the state capital. Lawmakers and other important people often stopped at the tavern for a drink or a bite to eat. There, they talked and argued about the issues of the day. Martin, quick and clever, listened and learned. Even as a child, his interest in politics was clear. No one imagined that this intelligent boy would one day reshape politics in the United States. No one could have dreamed that he would become the nation's eighth president.

Martin graduated from the village academy when he was fourteen years old. Even then, he knew what he wanted to do: study law. Martin's father helped him get a job in a local law office. The young man swept floors, ran errands, and did other chores. In his spare time, he read everything he could about the law.

▲ *Young Martin greatly admired Thomas Jefferson.*

Martin also learned as much as possible about future president Thomas Jefferson, who had been one of the nation's founders.

Jefferson was Martin's idol. Later in his political career, Van Buren tried to put Jefferson's ideals and beliefs into practice.

Van Buren completed his education in New York City. In 1803, he became a lawyer. The twenty-one-year-old then returned to Kinderhook. He began to build a name for himself. Intelligent and hardworking, Van Buren became known for taking on cases that other lawyers were afraid to tackle. He was soon a leading lawyer in the Hudson River valley.

Old City Hall in ▼ New York City at the time that Van Buren was studying to be a lawyer

As Van Buren did well, he developed a taste for the finer things in life. He enjoyed music and singing, and he often visited the theater. Van Buren also loved fine clothing. A short, handsome man with red, curly hair and clear blue eyes, "Little Van" cut a stylish figure in his expensive clothes.

▲ Hannah Hoes married Martin Van Buren in 1807.

In 1807, Van Buren married Hannah Hoes, a child-hood friend and distant cousin. Over the next ten years, the Van Burens had four sons: Abraham, John, Martin, and Smith Thompson. By all accounts, the Van Burens loved one another dearly.

The Young Politician

★ ★ ★

Van Buren was active in politics even before he became a lawyer. In 1801, when he was just nineteen years old, Van Buren joined the Democratic-Republican Party. At that time, it was one of two major political parties in the United States. The other was the Federalist Party. The Democratic-Republican Party had been founded by Thomas Jefferson in 1792. Today's Democratic Party traces its history to Jefferson's party.

As Van Buren became a successful lawyer, he attracted the

Martin Van Buren ▶
entered politics at
an early age.

attention of the party leaders. In 1808, they appointed Van Buren to a local office, the first of many political positions he would hold.

In 1812, Van Buren ran for the New York state senate and won. Four years later, he was reelected. While senator, Van Buren was appointed New York's **attorney general**.

As a senator, Van Buren worked to make many important changes in the state. He supported building the Erie Canal, which allowed ships to pass from the Atlantic Ocean to the Great Lakes. He also helped rewrite New York's constitution. The new constitution

◀ *The Erie Canal*

greatly improved New York's government. It doubled the number of people who could vote in the state. It also abolished, or did away with, many government jobs that were not needed.

Van Buren's success made him a powerful man in New York. However, that success earned him many enemies. Van Buren's enemies said that he was sly, scheming, and power hungry. They accused him of never taking a firm stand on any issue. They nicknamed him the "Little Magician" because he always seemed to come out on the winning side of every argument. Others called Van Buren the "Red Fox of Kinderhook" for his wily ways. These two nicknames followed Van Buren for the rest of his career.

One of Van Buren's most powerful enemies was De Witt Clinton, the Democratic-Republican governor of New York. In 1819, Clinton removed Van Buren as attorney general. This move caused a deep split within the Democratic-Republican Party. Some party members lined up behind Van Buren while others stood by the governor. Van Buren supporters were called Bucktails because they wore deer tails on their hats at meetings. By 1820, the Bucktails had taken firm control of New York's government.

During Van Buren's second term as state senator, disaster struck at home. In 1819, Hannah Hoes Van Buren died, possibly from tuberculosis, a disease that affects the lungs. In the early 1800s, tuberculosis was almost always

◄ *De Witt Clinton, governor of New York*

John Van Buren, ▶
the second son of
Martin Van Buren,
became a lawyer
like his father. He
was only a few
days shy of nine
years old when his
mother died.

deadly. After Hannah's death, Van Buren placed his sons in the care of relatives and concentrated on his career. Van Buren stayed in contact with his children and visited them during holidays. When he became president in 1836, all four of his sons came to live with him in the White House. Van Buren never remarried.

By the end of his second term as state senator, Martin Van Buren was one of the most powerful figures in New York politics. In 1821, Van Buren was elected to the U.S. Senate. The move was a big step up the ladder for the clever politician. Van Buren still wanted to keep a firm grip on politics in New York while he was away. Before he moved to Washington, he set up the Albany Regency. It was a group of politicians who supported Van Buren. They kept their power by granting favors or giving jobs to voters who supported them.

The Albany Regency was New York's first statewide **political machine**. For more than twenty years, the Albany Regency controlled politics in New York. Van Buren, far away in Washington, controlled the Albany Regency.

Onto the National Scene

★　★　★

Van Buren's reputation arrived in Washington, D.C., before he did. Politicians in the capital were already talking about the man who pulled the strings in New York. Once Van Buren settled in Washington in 1821, he went right to work. He soon became one of the most important politicians in Congress.

Construction on ▶ the Capitol in Washington was completed during Van Buren's time there as a U.S. senator.

As a U.S. senator, Van Buren supported **states' rights**. He believed that each state should have the right to govern itself—as long as it obeyed the U.S. Constitution. Van Buren was against politicians who wanted to take power away from the states and put it into the hands of the federal government.

The states' rights issue was closely tied to slavery, which was an issue dividing the nation. Many people in the North believed that slavery should be abolished throughout the United States. These people were called **abolitionists**. Slave owners in the South, however, believed that the South's economic well-being depended upon slavery. Most Southerners believed that each state should have the right to choose whether or not to allow slavery within its borders.

▼ *American writer William Lloyd Garrison was the founder of the abolitionist newspaper* The Liberator.

Southern plantation ▲
owners relied on
slaves to work their
large farms.

Martin Van Buren believed that slavery was wrong. He was against allowing slavery in any new state that was joining the Union. Yet Van Buren didn't think that the federal government had the power to do away with slavery in states where it already existed. To keep the country together, Van Buren believed it was important to find ways to make both Northerners and Southerners happy. Many people criticized Van Buren's "please everyone" attitude. Some began to call him a "professional politician." They said he cared only about gaining power for himself.

Van Buren couldn't understand these attacks. He always tried to be pleasant and polite, even toward his worst political enemies. He never lost his temper in public. In 1822, he wrote, "Why the deuce is it that they have such an itching for abusing me? I try to be harmless, and positively good natured, and a most decided friend of peace."

▼ *Slaves were bought and sold at auctions in the South.*

In fact, Van Buren did care about what was good for the public. For example, he worked to put an end to the tradition of debtor's prison. At the time, people who could not pay their taxes or other debts were locked up. In 1828, Van Buren helped pass a bill that outlawed jailing people for owing money.

In 1824, John Quincy Adams was elected president of the United States. Van Buren did not support Adams or his policies. Instead, he had thrown his support behind Andrew Jackson during the election. Jackson had become

Jailing those who ▼ owed money was a custom brought to the colonies from England. Fleet Prison in London (below) was mainly used for debtors.

a national hero during the War of 1812 (1812–1814) and had nearly beaten Adams to become president. Over the next four years, Van Buren worked hard to make Jackson the next U.S. president. He blocked many of President Adams's proposals. He also kept Jackson in the public eye.

Van Buren decided that the best way to get support for Jackson was to create a new political party. Called the

◄ *John Quincy Adams was the sixth president of the United States.*

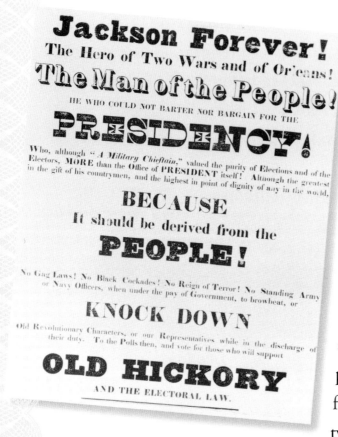

Jackson Forever!
The Hero of Two Wars and of Or'eans!
The Man of the People!
HE WHO COULD NOT BARTER NOR BARGAIN FOR THE
PRESIDENCY!
Who, although "*A Military Chieftain*," valued the purity of Elections and of the Electors, MORE than the Office of PRESIDENT itself! Although the greatest in the gift of his countrymen, and the highest in point of dignity of any in the world,

BECAUSE
It should be derived from the
PEOPLE!

No Gag Laws! No Black Cockades! No Reign of Terror! No Standing Army or Navy Officers, when under the pay of Government, to browbeat, or

KNOCK DOWN
Old Revolutionary Characters, or our Representatives while in the discharge of their duty. To the Polls then, and vote for those who will support

OLD HICKORY
AND THE ELECTORAL LAW.

An 1828 election poster for Andrew Jackson's presidential campaign

Democratic Party, this new group united both Northern and Southern politicians who were strong supporters of states' rights. In 1828, the Democratic Party nominated their first **candidates**: Andrew Jackson for president and John C. Calhoun, a prominent Southerner, for vice president. These two very different men ran against President John Quincy Adams. In fact, Calhoun had served as Adams's vice president.

To boost Jackson's chances of winning in the state of New York, Van Buren ran for governor there. When the votes were counted, both Jackson and Van Buren had won. In December 1828, Van Buren left the U.S. Senate and returned to New York to become governor.

The President's Right-Hand Man

★ ★ ★

Back in New York, Van Buren settled into his new job. During his first few weeks in office, he set up the Safety Fund System. This system required banks to join a special group. Each bank paid a yearly fee to join. Then, if one of the banks went out of business, the group made sure the bank's customers did not lose their money.

◀ *President Andrew Jackson rewarded Van Buren for his loyalty by making him one of his most trusted advisers.*

Although Van Buren was holding New York's top job, President Andrew Jackson had bigger plans for his loyal supporter. Less than three months after taking office, Van Buren was called back to Washington, D.C. Jackson rewarded Little Van by making him **secretary of state**. The secretary of state is the top government official in charge of foreign affairs. As secretary of state, Van Buren advised President Jackson on international issues. During his two years on the job, Van Buren worked out a trade **treaty** with Turkey. He also worked out treaties with Great Britain and France.

Van Buren quickly became one of President Jackson's most trusted advisers. He was the leader of the Kitchen Cabinet, an unofficial group of advisers who were completely loyal to Jackson. The president greatly valued Van Buren's honesty and intelligence. He thought of Van Buren as a "true man in whom there is no **guile**." When people criticized Van Buren as being a slick politician, Jackson defended his secretary of state. "It is said that he is a great magician," the president wrote. "I believe it, but his only wand is good common sense, which he uses for the benefit of the country."

Van Buren's strong ties to the president angered some politicians. One man who resented Van Buren's power was Vice President John C. Calhoun. He thought Van Buren was a "weasel." He hated that Van Buren had the president's trust and respect. Calhoun hoped to become president someday, and he wanted no competition for the top spot.

◄ *Vice President John C. Calhoun tried to end Van Buren's political career.*

In 1831, Van Buren stepped down as secretary of state. Jackson then appointed him **ambassador** to Great Britain. Neither Van Buren nor Jackson understood how deeply Calhoun disliked the powerful New Yorker. In January 1832, Congress voted on whether to approve Van Buren's appointment as ambassador. When there is a tie in the Senate, the vice president gets to vote. Vice President Calhoun cast the tie-breaking vote against Van Buren. Calhoun was thrilled. He believed that he had

Henry Clay ▲

ended Van Buren's political career forever. "It will kill him, sir, kill him dead," he said after voting against Jackson's right-hand man.

Jackson was furious at Calhoun. He insisted that the Democratic Party make Van Buren, not Calhoun, his running mate when he ran for reelection later that year. In 1832, Jackson and Van Buren easily defeated Kentucky politician Henry Clay in the election. The Dutchman from Kinderhook had become vice president of the United States.

As vice president, Van Buren continued to serve Jackson loyally. Van Buren did not agree with all of Jackson's decisions, but he always stood behind the president and supported him in public. Later, some of Jackson's poor decisions would come back to haunt Van Buren.

◀ *Martin Van Buren served faithfully as secretary of state and later as vice president.*

As President Jackson's second term was ending, he let the Democratic Party know that he wanted Van Buren to be their next candidate for president. The party followed the popular president's wishes. In 1836, Van Buren ran for president with Richard Johnson of Kentucky as his running mate.

During that election, Van Buren faced three Whig candidates. The Whigs were a new political party, formed in 1834 to oppose President Jackson and his policies. The party was so new that it was very disorganized. The Whigs could not decide upon one man to run against Van Buren. Instead, they chose someone from each section of the nation. Daniel Webster of Massachusetts ran

Van Buren's running mate Richard M. Johnson

in the North, Hugh Lawson White of Tennessee ran in the South, and William Henry Harrison of Indiana ran in the West. The Whigs hoped that each candidate would take enough votes away from Van Buren to send the election to the U.S. House of Representatives. If no one person received 50 percent of the vote, it would be up to the House to pick the next president.

◀ *Daniel Webster was one of three Whig Party candidates to run against Van Buren.*

Van Buren was tough to beat, however, because President Jackson was still very popular. As Jackson's right-hand man, the New Yorker enjoyed the support of voters across the nation. Van Buren also ran one of the first modern election **campaigns**. He used **slogans**, fund-raisers, and rallies. Clubs to support Van Buren sprang up everywhere. These clubs were known as OK clubs, for the initials for "Old Kinderhook." Soon, OK came to mean all right. Everywhere he spoke, Van Buren promised to "tread generally in the footsteps of President Jackson."

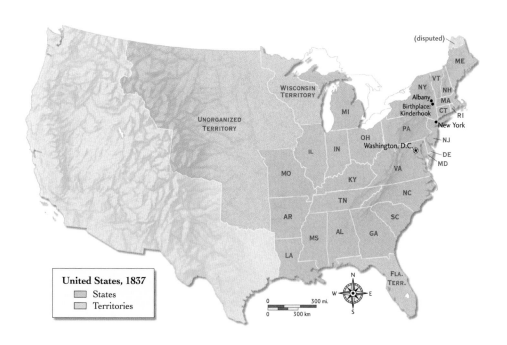

United States, 1837
☐ States
☐ Territories

Van Buren easily won the election. He collected more votes than the other three candidates combined. On the day Van Buren was sworn in as president, he and Jackson rode together to the Capitol.

▼ *The inauguration of Martin Van Buren took place on March 4, 1837.*

A Difficult Presidency

★ ★ ★

When Van Buren moved into the White House, he brought his four sons to Washington, D.C., to live with him. He hired his oldest son, Abraham, to act as his personal secretary. Despite the presence of four young men, many people felt that the Van Buren White House was a very dull place. Because Van Buren was a widower, there was no first lady to host parties and entertain.

Abraham Van Buren, Martin's oldest son and personal secretary ▶

Former first lady Dolley Madison was one person who thought the White House should be livelier. Soon after the Van Burens moved into the White House, Dolley introduced her young cousin Angelica Singleton to Abraham Van Buren. The two fell in love. They were married in 1838. For the rest of Van Buren's term, Angelica acted as her father-in-law's hostess. She succeeded in brightening up the White House.

◄ *Former first lady Dolley Madison (above) introduced Abraham Van Buren to Angelica Singleton (left).*

Just two months after taking office, Van Buren faced a serious national crisis. Beginning in May 1837, the country experienced its first economic **depression**. Across the nation, banks went out of business. Companies closed down, and people lost their jobs. Thousands lost their homes and went hungry as food prices soared.

General store customers faced large bills as food prices rose rapidly in 1837.

The Panic of 1837 was the worst economic disaster the United States had seen. In part, it was caused by former president Andrew Jackson's economic policies. With Jackson now gone, Americans turned to Van Buren for help and relief.

From May to September, however, Van Buren refused to act. He thought that the best course of action was to do nothing. He believed that given time, the economy would bounce back and recover on its own.

In September, Van Buren called a special session of Congress. He told Americans that they would not receive help from the federal government. He did not believe it was the government's role to help individuals.

Van Buren did act to make sure that the government's money stayed safe. He urged that federal funds be removed from state banks and kept by a central agency. In 1840, Van Buren's Independent Treasury System was finally passed by Congress. This treasury system was among the president's major accomplishments in office.

The days and months wore on, and the economy did not recover on its own. In fact, the crisis only got worse. The depression, which lasted nearly five years, turned many citizens against Van Buren. They thought that he

Many people saw Van Buren as a president who did not care about the welfare of Americans.

should have acted more quickly to stop the economic slump and help the American people.

More and more, Van Buren came under attack. His political enemies labeled him as a man who did not care about the common people. They made fun of his fancy clothing and mocked his special carriage drawn by matching horses. Americans soon were calling Van Buren by a new name: Martin Van Ruin.

Van Buren was also criticized for the way he dealt with Native Americans. Before Van Buren took office, President Jackson had ordered thousands of Native Americans off their tribal lands in the South. They were to move west of the Mississippi River to Indian Territory. At that time, Indian Territory included what is now Oklahoma and parts of Kansas and Nebraska. Many people were outraged by Jackson's order. The U.S. Supreme Court even told Jackson that he had no right to force the Native Americans to move west.

Van Buren, however, carried out Jackson's wishes. During his term, more than 13,000 Cherokee people were forced to march more than 800 miles (1,287 kilometers) from Georgia to Indian Territory. More than 4,000 died along the way, and the march became known as the Trail of Tears. Van Buren also continued the war, begun by Jackson, against the Seminole people in Florida. The war cost the government $40 million and caused the deaths of thousands of American soldiers and Seminole Indians.

▾ *A painting of the Trail of Tears by Robert Lindneux*

Van Buren was also faulted for the way he handled international problems. In 1839, fighting broke out along the border between the United States and Canada. Known as the Aroostook War, the conflict began when American and Canadian loggers both claimed the Aroostook Valley, a piece of land near the border, as their own. Both sides believed that they should control the area's thick forests.

The U.S. Congress wanted war. Congress approved sending money and troops to take control of the valley. Van Buren, however, preferred "peace with honor." He ordered

A battle during ▼ the Seminole War

U.S. troops to the border, but only to prevent any violence. In time, both sides agreed to stop fighting. Van Buren had kept the United States out of a war that could have been long and costly. Still, many Americans believed that the president had been timid and weak.

Van Buren did have some success as president. He developed the Independent Treasury System. He also took action to protect workers. For instance, in 1840, Van Buren ordered that people working on federal public works projects could work no more than ten hours each day.

▼ *A satirical cartoon about the rising tensions during the Aroostook war*

THE MAIN QUESTION.

Defeat and Retirement

★   ★   ★

Despite the criticism of Van Buren, the Democrats chose him to run for a second term as president. This time, Van Buren campaigned without a running mate. Few people liked Vice President Richard Johnson, and he was not given the chance to run for another term. Van Buren is the only U.S. president who campaigned without a vice presidential candidate.

Van Buren's opponent during the election of 1840 was Whig candidate William Henry Harrison. Van Buren had beaten Harrison in 1836, but this time, the Whigs were ready for a fight. They ran a lively campaign, complete with parades, parties, brass bands, and bonfires. They presented their candidate as a man of the people, someone who had led a simple life and had been born in a log cabin. Harrison was, in fact, the son of a rich Virginia planter.

◄ William Henry Harrison was the ninth president of the United States.

The Whigs were quick to criticize Van Buren. They accused him of having no feeling or concern for the common man. One Whig campaign slogan was, "Van, Van, is a used up man."

The Whigs' campaign strategy paid off, and Harrison easily defeated Van Buren. Although he did not know it yet, Van Buren's political career had come to an end.

After his defeat, Van Buren retired to Lindenwald, a home he had bought near Kinderhook. The former president began farming, growing fruit, vegetables, and wheat. He also kept adding to and improving his home.

At Lindenwald, Van Buren made plans to win back the presidency. Most people expected that the New Yorker would be the Democratic candidate for president in 1844. Van Buren, however, disagreed with his party on one important issue: Texas. While most Democrats wanted to add Texas to the United States, Van Buren did

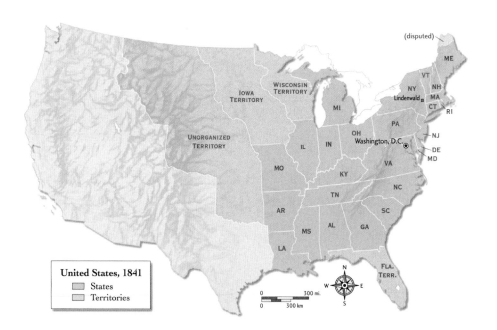

United States, 1841
States
Territories

not. He believed that adding Texas as a state would spread slavery and cause a war with Mexico. Unhappy with this view, the Democrats passed over Van Buren and chose James K. Polk as their candidate. Polk, who wanted to add Texas to U.S. territory, went on to win the election.

During the 1848 election, Van Buren tried again. This time he was the candidate for the Free-Soil Party. It had been founded in 1848 to oppose the spread of slavery. Van Buren's running mate was Charles Francis Adams, the son of Little Van's former political rival John Quincy Adams. Van Buren did not win this election either, but he did receive 10 percent of the vote.

◀ *A campaign poster for Van Buren's 1848 Free-Soil Party showing Van Buren (left) and Charles Francis Adams*

After this final defeat, Van Buren traveled to Europe. In Italy, he began working on his autobiography. Van Buren returned to New York in 1854, where he lived in peace and comfort with his sons and their families. One of the many people who admired the former president was author Washington Irving. He thought highly of Van Buren. Irving said, "The more I see of Mr. Van Buren the more I feel confirmed in a strong personal regard for him. He is one of the gentlest and most amiable men I have ever met with."

Author Washington Irving (above) greatly admired Van Buren (below).

Even in his later years, Van Buren remained interested in U.S. politics. He supported Franklin Pierce and James Buchanan in their bids to be president. Although Van Buren did not support Abraham Lincoln when he ran for president, he did support Lincoln's actions after he was elected.

In July 1862, Van Buren suffered a serious **asthma** attack and began to weaken rapidly. On July 24, he died at Lindenwald. He was seventy-nine years old. At Van Buren's funeral, eighty-one carriages followed his coffin to the cemetery.

◀ Van Buren named his home Lindenwald (Linden Woods) after the trees that grew on the property.

Martin Van Buren was not one of the greatest presidents in U.S. history. His one term was marked by severe economic depression and other serious conflicts. Van Buren was proud of his four years as the leader of

Martin Van Buren was buried in his hometown of Kinderhook, New York. A stone obelisk marks his grave.

the United States, however. He believed that he had stayed true to his ideals and that he had acted in the best interests of the nation as a whole. He held the nation together at home and kept it out of war. In Andrew Jackson's words, Van Buren was a true friend of the people.

GLOSSARY

★ ★ ★

abolitionists—people who supported the banning of slavery

ambassador—the representative of a nation's government in another country

asthma—a lung disorder that makes it difficult to breathe

attorney general—the top lawyer for a state or nation

campaigns—efforts to win elections

candidates—people running for office in elections

depression—a time when businesses do badly and many people become poor

Dutch—people from the Netherlands; the language they speak

guile—dishonesty or trickery

political machine—a group of people who control a political party

secretary of state—a president's leading adviser in dealing with other countries

slogans—phrases used to capture public attention in a campaign

states' rights—the idea that all powers not given to the federal government in the U.S. Constitution belong to the states

treaty—an agreement between two governments

MARTIN VAN BUREN'S LIFE AT A GLANCE

★ ★ ★

PERSONAL

Nicknames:	Little Van, the Little Magician, the Red Fox of Kinderhook, Martin Van Ruin
Born:	December 5, 1782
Birthplace:	Kinderhook, New York
Father's name:	Abraham Van Buren
Mother's name:	Maria Hoes Van Buren
Education:	Graduated from Kinderhook Academy in 1796
Wife's name:	Hannah Hoes Van Buren (1783–1819)
Married:	February 21, 1807
Children:	Abraham Van Buren (1807–1873); John Van Buren (1810–1866); Martin Van Buren (1812–1855); Smith Thompson Van Buren (1817–1876)
Died:	July 24, 1862, in Kinderhook, New York
Buried:	Kinderhook Cemetery in Kinderhook, New York

PUBLIC

Occupation before presidency:	Lawyer, politician
Occupation after presidency:	Politician
Military service:	None
Other government positions:	New York state senator; attorney general of New York; U.S. senator from New York; governor of New York; secretary of state; vice president
Political party:	Democrat
Vice president:	Richard M. Johnson (1837–1841)
Dates in office:	March 4, 1837–March 3, 1841
Presidential opponents:	William Henry Harrison (Whig), Daniel Webster (Whig), Hugh Lawson White (Whig), 1836; William Henry Harrison (Whig), 1840
Number of votes (Electoral College):	764,176 of 1,502,300 (170 of 294), 1836; 1,127,781 of 2,402,405 (60 of 294), 1840
Writings:	*Inquiry into the Origin and Course of Political Parties in the United States* (1867); *The Autobiography of Martin Van Buren* (1920)

★

Martin Van Buren's Cabinet

Secretary of state:
John Forsyth (1837–1841)

Secretary of the treasury:
Levi Woodbury (1837–1841)

Secretary of war:
Joel R. Poinsett (1837–1841)

Attorney general:
Benjamin F. Butler (1837–1838)
Felix Grundy (1838–1839)
Henry D. Gilpin (1840–1841)

Postmaster general:
Amos Kendall (1837–1840)
John M. Niles (1840–1841)

Secretary of the navy:
Mahlon Dickerson (1837–1838)
James K. Paulding (1838–1841)

MARTIN VAN BUREN'S LIFE AND TIMES

★ ★ ★

VAN BUREN'S LIFE

WORLD EVENTS

1780

December 5,   1782
Van Buren
is born in
Kinderhook,
New York

1783   American author
Washington Irving
is born

1791   Austrian composer
Wolfgang Amadeus
Mozart (below) dies

VAN BUREN'S LIFE

WORLD EVENTS

1792   The dollar currency is introduced to America

1799   Napoléon Bonaparte (below) takes control of France

1803 Begins practicing law in New York

1800

1801   Ultraviolet radiation is discovered

1805   General anesthesia is first used in surgery

February 21, marries Hannah Hoes (below) 1807

1807   Robert Fulton's *Clermont* (below) is the first reliable steamship to travel between New York City and Albany

VAN BUREN'S LIFE

WORLD EVENTS

1809   American poet and short-story writer Edgar Allen Poe is born in Boston

1810   Bernardo O'Higgins (below) leads Chile in its fight for independence from Spain

Elected to the New York state senate   1812

1812–1814   The United States and Britain fight the War of 1812

Serves as the attorney general of New York   1815–1819

1814–1815   European states meet in Vienna, Austria, to redraw national borders after the conclusion of the Napoleonic Wars

1820

1820   Susan B. Anthony (below), a leader of the American woman suffrage movement, is born

Becomes a U.S. senator from New York   1821

★

VAN BUREN'S LIFE

WORLD EVENTS

1821   Central American countries gain independence from Spain

1823   Mexico becomes a republic

1826   The first photograph is taken by Joseph Niépce, a French physicist

1827   Modern-day matches are invented by coating the end of a wooden stick with phosphorus

Elected governor of New York   1828

Appointed secretary of state by President Andrew Jackson   1829

1829   The first practical sewing machine is invented by French tailor Barthélemy Thimonnier (below)

1830

Appointed ambassador to Great Britain, but the Senate refuses to confirm him   1831

Elected Andrew Jackson's vice president   1832

VAN BUREN'S LIFE

Presidential Election Results:	Popular Votes	Electoral Votes
1836 Martin Van Buren	764,176	170
William H. Harrison	550,816	73
Hugh L. White	146,107	26
Daniel Webster	41,201	14
W. P. Mangum	–	11

1837   May 10, the Panic of 1837, the nation's first major economic depression, begins

1838–1839   Cherokee Indians from the southeastern United States are forced to march 800 miles (1,287 km) to Indian Territory in the Trail of Tears

1839   Fighting breaks out on the border between Canada and the United States in what becomes known as the Aroostook War

WORLD EVENTS

1833   Great Britain abolishes slavery

1836   Texans defeat Mexican troops at San Jacinto after a deadly battle at the Alamo (below)

1837   American banker J. P. Morgan is born

1838   The Boers defeat the Zulus in the Battle of Blood River in Natal

1839   The Opium War between China and Great Britain begins

VAN BUREN'S LIFE				WORLD EVENTS	

VAN BUREN'S LIFE

Federal treasury created to protect the government's money — 1840

Runs for reelection but loses

Fails to become the Democratic candidate for president — 1844

Runs for president as a member of the Free-Soil Party but loses — 1848

Civil War erupts between the Northern and Southern states — 1861–1865

July 24, Van Buren dies in Kinderhook, New York — 1862

WORLD EVENTS

1840 — Auguste Rodin, famous sculptor of *The Thinker* (below), is born

1848 — *The Communist Manifesto*, by German writer Karl Marx, is widely distributed

1852 — American Harriet Beecher Stowe publishes *Uncle Tom's Cabin*

1858 — English scientist Charles Darwin (below) presents his theory of evolution

Timeline markers: 1840, 1850, 1860

UNDERSTANDING MARTIN VAN BUREN AND HIS PRESIDENCY

★ ★ ★

IN THE LIBRARY

Ferry, Steven. *Martin Van Buren: Our Eighth President.*
Chanhassen, Minn.: The Child's World, 2002.

Hargrove, Jim. *Martin Van Buren: Eighth President of the
United States.* Chicago: Childrens Press, 1987.

Jankowski, Susan. *Martin Van Buren.* Berkeley Heights,
N.J.: MyReportLinks.com Books, 2002.

Welsbacher, Anne. *Martin Van Buren.*
Minneapolis: Abdo & Daughters, 2001.

ON THE WEB

FactHound offers a safe, fun way to find Internet sites
related to this book. All of the sites on FactHound
have been researched by our staff.

Here's all you do:
Visit *www.facthound.com*
FactHound will fetch the best sites for you!

VAN BUREN HISTORIC SITES ACROSS THE COUNTRY

Martin Van Buren National Historic Site
1013 Old Post Road
Kinderhook, NY 12106
518/758-6986
http://www.nps.gov/mava
To see the home and farm where
Van Buren lived after his presidency

THE U.S. PRESIDENTS
(Years in Office)

★ ★ ★

1. **George Washington**
   (March 4, 1789-March 3, 1797)
2. **John Adams**
   (March 4, 1797-March 3, 1801)
3. **Thomas Jefferson**
   (March 4, 1801-March 3, 1809)
4. **James Madison**
   (March 4, 1809-March 3, 1817)
5. **James Monroe**
   (March 4, 1817-March 3, 1825)
6. **John Quincy Adams**
   (March 4, 1825-March 3, 1829)
7. **Andrew Jackson**
   (March 4, 1829-March 3, 1837)
8. **Martin Van Buren**
   (March 4, 1837-March 3, 1841)
9. **William Henry Harrison**
   (March 6, 1841-April 4, 1841)
10. **John Tyler**
    (April 6, 1841-March 3, 1845)
11. **James K. Polk**
    (March 4, 1845-March 3, 1849)
12. **Zachary Taylor**
    (March 5, 1849-July 9, 1850)
13. **Millard Fillmore**
    (July 10, 1850-March 3, 1853)
14. **Franklin Pierce**
    (March 4, 1853-March 3, 1857)
15. **James Buchanan**
    (March 4, 1857-March 3, 1861)
16. **Abraham Lincoln**
    (March 4, 1861-April 15, 1865)
17. **Andrew Johnson**
    (April 15, 1865-March 3, 1869)

18. **Ulysses S. Grant**
    (March 4, 1869-March 3, 1877)
19. **Rutherford B. Hayes**
    (March 4, 1877-March 3, 1881)
20. **James Garfield**
    (March 4, 1881-Sept 19, 1881)
21. **Chester Arthur**
    (Sept 20, 1881-March 3, 1885)
22. **Grover Cleveland**
    (March 4, 1885-March 3, 1889)
23. **Benjamin Harrison**
    (March 4, 1889-March 3, 1893)
24. **Grover Cleveland**
    (March 4, 1893-March 3, 1897)
25. **William McKinley**
    (March 4, 1897-
    September 14, 1901)
26. **Theodore Roosevelt**
    (September 14, 1901-
    March 3, 1909)
27. **William Howard Taft**
    (March 4, 1909-March 3, 1913)
28. **Woodrow Wilson**
    (March 4, 1913-March 3, 1921)
29. **Warren G. Harding**
    (March 4, 1921-August 2, 1923)
30. **Calvin Coolidge**
    (August 3, 1923-March 3, 1929)
31. **Herbert Hoover**
    (March 4, 1929-March 3, 1933)
32. **Franklin D. Roosevelt**
    (March 4, 1933-April 12, 1945)

33. **Harry S. Truman**
    (April 12, 1945-
    January 20, 1953)
34. **Dwight D. Eisenhower**
    (January 20, 1953-
    January 20, 1961)
35. **John F. Kennedy**
    (January 20, 1961-
    November 22, 1963)
36. **Lyndon B. Johnson**
    (November 22, 1963-
    January 20, 1969)
37. **Richard M. Nixon**
    (January 20, 1969-
    August 9, 1974)
38. **Gerald R. Ford**
    (August 9, 1974-
    January 20, 1977)
39. **James Earl Carter**
    (January 20, 1977-
    January 20, 1981)
40. **Ronald Reagan**
    (January 20, 1981-
    January 20, 1989)
41. **George H. W. Bush**
    (January 20, 1989-
    January 20, 1993)
42. **William Jefferson Clinton**
    (January 20, 1993-
    January 20, 2001)
43. **George W. Bush**
    (January 20, 2001-)

INDEX

★ ★ ★

ABOUT THE AUTHOR

Robin S. Doak has been writing for children for more than fourteen years. A former editor of *Weekly Reader* and *U*S*Kids* magazine, Ms. Doak has authored fun and educational materials for kids of all ages. Some of her work includes biographies of explorers such as Henry Hudson and John Smith, as well as other titles in this series. Ms. Doak is a past winner of an Educational Press Association of America Distinguished Achievement Award. She lives with her husband and three children in central Connecticut.